HINTS

FOR

IMPROVING THE CONDITION

OF THE

PEASANTRY.

HINTS

FOR

IMPROVING THE CONDITION

OF THE

PEASANTRY

IN ALL PARTS OF THE

UNITED KINGDOM,

BY PROMOTING COMFORT IN THEIR HABITATIONS:

INTERSPERSED WITH

PLANS, ELEVATIONS, AND DESCRIPTIVE VIEWS

OF CHARACTERISTIC

DESIGNS for COTTAGES,

CONTRIVED FOR

THE USE AND CONVENIENCE OF THE PEASANT AND SMALL FARMER, AS WELL AS OCCASIONAL RETREATS FOR PERSONS OF MODERATE INCOME.

ILLUSTRATED ON

TEN PLATES,

HANDSOMELY ENGRAVED IN AQUATINTA, AND EMBELLISHED WITH PICTURESQUE SCENERY, ELEGANTLY COLOURED TO IMITATE THE DRAWINGS.

TO WHICH ARE PREFIXED,

Introductory Observations on the cheapest, best, and most approved Manner
OF
BUILDING THEM,

Under the impression that the Materials of every Description will be found by the Landed Proprietor.

TO WHICH ARE ADDED,
EXPLANATIONS AND ESTIMATES MADE ACCORDINGLY.

———

By RICHARD ELSAM,

ARCHITECT,

AUTHOR OF "AN ESSAY ON RURAL ARCHITECTURE," &c.

———

—— " A BOLD PEASANTRY, THEIR COUNTRY'S PRIDE,
" WHEN ONCE DESTROY'D, CAN NEVER BE SUPPLIED."
GOLDSMITH.

———

Printed for and Published by R. Ackermann, No. 101, Strand;
AND MAY BE HAD OF
THE AUTHOR, 15, SOUTHAMPTON ROW, RUSSELL SQUARE.

1816.

ISBN 0 576 15162 9

Republished in 1971 by Gregg International Publishers Limited
Westmead, Farnborough, Hants., England.

Printed in Offset by Kingprint Limited
Richmond, Surrey, England.

TO

THOMAS WILLIAM COKE, Esq.

OF

HOLKHAM,

MEMBER OF PARLIAMENT

FOR THE

County of Norfolk,

THIS WORK,

ENCOURAGED BY HIS FAVOR AND HONORED BY HIS PATRONAGE,

IS DEDICATED,

AS THE

FRIEND OF THE PEASANT AND PROMOTER OF AGRICULTURE,

BY

HIS MOST OBEDIENT AND MOST HUMBLE SERVANT,

RICHARD ELSAM.

TO THE READER.

———

THIS work embraces a general view of our peasantry in all parts of the united kingdom, with the causes of their distress in certain districts, as also the ulterior advantages that may be expected by the kingdom at large, and in particular by the landed and agricultural interest uniting to promote the comfort, health, morals, and condition of those useful members of the community; at the same time introducing a more characteristic style of building their habitations than at present prevails. In studying designs of this description, simplicity, utility, and economy are the chief points to be considered; and if, consistently with these ideas, a portion of interest can be produced, it is a proof of good sense to encourage their adoption in situations where they are likely to inspire the rising generation with a spirit for improving the general appearance of the country. With the intention of cultivating these principles, and of improving the condition of the peasantry, the following work has been undertaken; and, in the hope of rendering it still more useful and interesting, the plans have been so arranged, that they may be converted at a small expence into occasional retreats for persons with moderate incomes. The designs are select, but few in number, and consist of plans, elevations, and descriptive views, which have been drawn, and redrawn to large and small scales, and are handsomely engraved in aquatinta upon ten plates, which are coloured to illustrate their general effects, combined with picturesque scenery: to which are prefixed, introductory observations on the cheapest, best, and most approved manner of building them ; concluding with illustrative explanations and estimates, made according to the average prices of labor, exclusive of the materials, which in all cases are presumed to be found by the landed proprietors. Many of the suggestions contained in this little work, owe their origin to various conversations with country gentlemen intimately acquainted with the state of agriculture, as well as the condition of the peasantry in the parts where they reside ; which, together with a variety of miscellaneous information obtained upon the subject, in a series of journies through the different parts of the united kingdom, has given birth to the present publication ; in contemplating which, the principal object has been to improve the condition of our numerous and interesting peasantry ; and in order that country gentlemen, with the assistance of their agents, stewards, or bailiffs, may be enabled to carry any of the following designs into execution, without further instructions. An additional plate is given to the number before mentioned, which will fully explain the manner of finishing the windows, external doors, chimney stacks, and fire-places, so as to produce comfort, as well as the most pleasing and picturesque effects : but should any further instructions be required, the author will feel great pleasure in giving such information as may be requisite. And from having been engaged near thirty years in various parts of the kingdom, in designing and estimating public and private buildings, as well as improvements and additions to country seats, in the Grecian, Roman, Gothic, and Castle styles of building, he is induced to embrace the present opportunity of stating, that he will be happy to assist such gentlemen as may be about to build, and to furnish all sorts of plans, with such written instructions as may be necessary for the execution of their intended works ; and if required, he will be happy occasionally to superintend them, in order to give directions from time to time, as well as to measure and value the several works during their progress.

HINTS

FOR

IMPROVING THE CONDITION

OF THE

PEASANTRY.

NOW the blessings of peace are restored to these happy isles by the united efforts of our countrymen, who have bled in the field of battle to protect our civil rights and independence, it is the happy moment when we should turn our eyes towards the condition of the poor, and in particular to our interesting peasantry, whose comfort in every part of the united kingdom at the present period either more or less calls for attention; and, as monarchs, statesmen, and philosophers in all ages have concurred in opinion, that the riches of a nation are the people, and as the peasantry constitute so considerable a portion of our wealth, it is doubtless the duty of those in whose hands Providence has placed the means, to assist in promoting their welfare. The comforts and advantages derived in society by their laborious exertions, make it absolutely necessary that the greatest pains should be taken to improve their condition. It is therefore a subject of deep concern, that the miserable state of their habitations in many parts of these countries have never been seriously taken into consideration.

Peasants cottages are the habitations of rural labourers, and may be designed to create considerate interest: they are in general detached buildings on the estates of men of fortune, in the vicinity of the family mansion, or country villa: sometimes they compose entire villages or hamlets, and frequently present the most pleasing assemblage of picturesque buildings, as well as the most happy scenes in human life;

> ———— " Where cheerful guests retire,
> " To pause from toil, and trim their evening fire.
> *   *   *   *   *
> " Where all the ruddy family around,
> " Laugh at the jests, or pranks, that never fail,
> " Or sigh with sorrow at some mournful tale."

In various parts of the kingdom numerous examples of these buildings present themselves to view, not less admirable for their exterior beauty and situations, than for their interior neatness, comfort, and contrivance; and the care with which they are in some places preserved, blended with the fertile scenery of the country, convey to the spectator the most pleasurable sensations. But in many parts of the united kingdom these habitations are the most miserable huts that can be described. The traveller is however in some degree compensated for this disappointment, by the greatest variety of wild and romantic scenery; but, as the friend of mankind, anxious for the welfare and comfort of his fellow-creatures, he cannot but lament the fate of many thousands who, in these hospitable isles, are destined to live under hovels fit only to shelter the inhabitants of the forest from the inclemencies of the weather; nor is there any hope of extensive improvement, unless the landed proprietors in all parts of these countries could be induced generally to reside on their estates, and in the midst of those to whose industrious applications they are so much indebted; then, and not till then, can we hope to see the fruitful vallies, rich glens, and mountain scenery throughout these fertile countries clothed with peasants in comely attire, and in the occupation of cottages suited to their humble stations.

> " Ill fares the land, to hastening ills a prey,
> " Where wealth accumulates, and men decay.
> " Princes or lords may flourish or may fade,
> " A breath can make them, as a breath has made;
> " But a bold peasantry, their country's pride,
> " When once destroy'd, can never be supplied."

To observe our fellow-creatures employed in carrying on any occupation in which we are interested, and performing their services with cheerfulness and alacrity, is a rich source of gratification to a liberal and feeling mind, well worthy of being purchased by acts of benevolence, approbation, and reward. In taking this view of our subject therefore, it appears to be not only the moral put political duty of those who are the proprietors of large estates, if possible, to reside upon them, and by every means in their power to cultivate the friendship of the peasantry, by embracing every opportunity of improving their condition; and in those parts of the united kingdom where the nobility interest themselves to this effect, the comforts and advantages in society are obvious to the community at large.

To preserve health, to promote the comforts of the labouring classes in society, and to save numbers from an untimely grave, are objects of interest to the parent, the politician, and man of feeling. In every point of view, therefore, it appears incumbent on those who are prevented from residing on their estates, and whose ample fortunes will permit them to improve the condition of the peasantry, not only by causing suitable habitations to be erected for their comfort, but in allowing them such advantages as will enable them to bring up their families with comfort in the principles of morality, virtue, and religion.

And to the resident proprietor who enjoys the means, how pleasant must be the task of commencing an undertaking, whose end is to promote the happiness of those useful members of society, and at the same time to improve his estate; and how happy must he feel in the bosom of those whose comforts have been studied, and who have been raised by his benevolence from a state of misery to that of comparative independence.

To see the cottages in the neighbourhood of opulence clean and comfortable is most creditable, and, besides the gratification it affords, it has the sanction of good policy; it is likewise a great temptation to peasants with clean and industrious habits to seek such situations; the holders of land therefore may, with very little expence and trouble, have the most respectable labourers in the country. The cost of having these habitations annually repaired and white-washed, is but trifling, and contributes not only to comfort, but to health.

A farther attention to the cottager's comfort is attended with but little expence: a small garden well planted with fruit trees, as well as the walls of the cottage, will afford not only wholesome food for the family, but the surplus being sold, will procure other necessaries; and, with regard to the time requisite for cultivation, it will not break in upon his labour, nor will it in any degree tend to injure or oppress him.

Where it occurs, which is frequently the case, that the peasants have to traverse over considerable tracts of land to arrive at their work, the loss is great, as it takes up a large portion of their time, independent of what is requisite for rest and proper relaxation. Now, as half an hour lost in the work any labourer in the course of a year amounts to a fortnight's labour, it is certainly worthy of consideration in all great concerns, if possible, to avoid this evil by suitable arrangements: it is therefore much to the advantage of the agriculturist to have his labourers reside in the adjoining village, or as near to the farm as possible, to receive orders, in case the weather or other circumstances should require an alteration in the plan of labour for the day; but where the land intended for cultivation, or the work to be performed, is at a distance, detached cottages are indispensable; in which case, the greatest pains should be taken to select the best and most picturesque situations, in order that when grouped with judicious plantations, they may become objects of interest in the various rides through the domain; and, for the comfort of the peasant, in disposing of the apartments, great care should be taken to avoid the keen blasts of the northern wind, and to embrace all the local advantages of warm and genial aspects, that when the weary peasant retires from the toils of the day, he may sit himself down to his humble fare, the monarch of his mansion, and enjoy the endearing smiles of his family in the cheering presence of the setting sun.

We have the best authority for stating, that it is not only practicable, but within the power of every country gentleman, to create a spirit of enthusiasm in those whom he employs, and to turn it to the best of purposes. In some parts it may be a difficult undertaking, but the difficulty constitutes the merit. It may not be the work of a short period, but that a system may be established for bringing it about cannot be disputed. The plan proposed, and which we understand has received the sanction of some of the first agriculturists, on the recomendation of a most worthy and patriotic improver, is the TAKING APPRENTICES SONS OF THE PEASANTRY, which might be easily and advantageously done in every large farming establishment; a certain but moderate degree of education suitable to their future employment, as well as their quickness of comprehension, would be necessary; and their rise and confidence should be gradual, and altogether proportioned to their exertions. In lads it is no difficult matter to create a spirit of emulation and rivalship, and this directed to proper objects, would scarce fail of rendering them valuable servants during their time of service, and afterwards useful members of society. This is not suggested as a mere speculative opinion, but one which has been acted upon for many years in the north of England, where, if the apprentices conduct themselves to the satisfaction of their employers, on the expiration of of their indentures they receive a present of ten guineas, or more; but this entirely depends on their own good conduct. They are instructed in reading, writing, and arithmetic, which not only enables them to acquire a more perfect knowledge of the business they are engaged in, but fits them afterwards to establish themselves, and to be able to turn to their own advantage what they have seen practised from their earliest days. No plan appears better calculated than this for improving the condition of the peasantry, or for more generally diffusing experimental knowledge in agriculture. And if all the great landed proprietors throughout the empire were once to take this subject into their serious consideration, there is little doubt but the prevalence of the example would quickly take effect, and that the peasantry throughout these countries in the course of a few years would be superior to any in the world.

To obtain general information on this subject, the traveller must expect and be prepared to witness the greatest scenes of distress, particularly in some parts of the kingdom, where the sorrows of many thousands can be alleviated in no other way than by ameliorating the sufferings of the peasantry, who in their present habitations are destitute of the most common comforts of life; and these remarks are made in the ardent hope they may prove useful in bettering their condition : the knowledge of whose situation has been acquired by visiting their habitations, and inquiring into particulars which, though they would be tedious and uninteresting in detail, are of importance in the consideration of plans intended for their comfort.

Now as these useful and interesting members of the community have in general large families, it is absolutely necessary they should be provided with more than one sleeping room, independent of a spacious kitchen, with a roomy and comfortable fire place : and this observation is made in consequence of remarking, that it is a very common circumstance to find poor cottagers in the occupation of huts, with a considerable number in family, crowded together in one room, with a cow, a pig, and sometimes a quantity of poultry, with no other aperture than a door in a mud wall to let out the smoke. Surely nothing can be more pernicious to the health, or more injurious to the morals, than this mode of living; yet it is to be lamented that in many parts of the united kingdom the condition of the peasantry is much worse than it is here described. In plans, therefore, intended for their comfort the greatest care should be taken to avoid the evil complained of by dividing the interior of the spaces, to be occupied in such manner, that with greater facility the apartments may at any time be subdivided, to make provision for children as they progressively advance to maturity.

Where an interest is taken in the welfare of the peasantry, they are in general sober, honest, and industrious, careful of their families, neat and clean in their persons and habitations, humble and dutiful to their superiors, happy and content in their stations, punctual in discharge of their moral obligations, and constant in their attendance at divine service; nor are they less proud of their situations than prompt in compliance with the wishes of their employers; but where they are treated with neglect, which is almost invariably the case in the sister country, their habits, manners, and general conduct is the reverse of what we have described, and their ruinous habitations the most deplorable scenes of misery and distress; yet, notwithstanding their treatment, when called upon to assist in defending the interests of the empire at large, they never fail in conjunction with the best of troops, boldly to manifest their loyalty and attachment in the field of battle. By their toil and their blood they have in every part of the world contributed to maintain the pride, honour, and independence of the British empire. Under these circumstances we cannot but sincerely lament, that their comforts and general condition in society have never been fairly taken into consideration by the friends of humanity in either of the houses of parliament.

It is true that numerous plans for their education have been devised with the best of motives; but it is in vain to think we can improve their minds when we neglect their bodies; for, who ever heard of a people desirous of education, who had not clothes to cover them, bread to eat, or houses fit to shelter them from the inclemencies of the weather? nor can it be expected that people under such circumstances have any appetites for moral instructions.

How the owners of the soil can therefore reconcile it to their feelings or to their interests, to remain silent spectators of the present state of things, or how they can refrain from the pleasure of setting the example upon their estates, of building suitable cottages for improving the condition of the peasantry, is a subject of universal surprise.

By the landed proprietors residing upon their estates, and reletting their farms at moderate rents proportioned to the times, and by various acts of kindness, it is in their power to be of infinite service.   These are the natural and most amiable remedies for the discontents of the peasantry in that part of the kingdom, which, if put into practice, would speedily conciliate their affections, and render them tranquil and happy,   But, alas! the poor unfortunate creatures in most parts of that neglected country are treated with so much indifference, that in cases of the slightest commotion, they seldom fail to manifest their sentiments by conduct which make it absolutely necessary for the government of the country to resort to coercive measures, the painful but urgent necessity for which is generally created by local disputes among the small farmers or peasants about tithes, renewals of leases, or grievances of minor importance, which might be redressed by the interference and presence of their landlords, who it is natural for them to hope and to consider as their friends and benefactors; and it is in consequence of a succession of such disturbances, that few people think of visiting that part of the united kingdom except upon business, or to view the romantic beauties of the county of Wicklow, the enchanting lakes of Killarney, or the still more wonderful and stupendous rocks of the Giant's Causeway; and those who are induced to take this tour, generally set out with so many unfortunate prejudices on their minds, that they seldom tarry long : and for these reasons, generally speaking, the people of England are not so much acquainted with that part of the united kingdom as with many others, and foreigners are still less, for it being in some degree a remote country, that is, from its not being in the direct way to any other, is seldom visited by them ; but, for its numerous and abundant population, internal riches, and general importance, it is of inestimable value.   In a country, therefore, where the opulent and respectable inhabitants are so much reputed for their hospitality, it is to be regretted, that a bold and interesting peasantry, the pride, ornament, and strength of a nation, should be no better provided for.   It is however worthy of observation, that although the poor laws do not extend to it, yet, independent of the county infirmaries and other public charities, collections are weekly made in the different parish churches, which are regularly distributed to the most deserving, under the direction of the ministers and churchwardens.   Nor is it less worthy of observation, that in some districts where the land-owners reside, that the condition of the peasants cottages are superior to the general view we have before taken of them, and that the peasantry are much better attended to, particularly in cases of sickness or distress, where their wants are taken into consideration with the greatest humanity and attention, and under circumstances which reflect the greatest honor upon the ladies of a certain rank in the country, who are in most places tolerably well versed in the simple compounds of medicine, which they distribute to the labouring poor, accompanied with the most friendly advice.

The pleasing effects of order and industry, when combined with plenty, must always afford ample gratification to the benevolent mind, and in particular to those entrusted with the happiness of the inferior orders of society. When we therefore see wretched and dirty cottages, miserable and dilapidated farms, upon good but ill-cultivated ground, scantily stocked with poor cattle, what are the sensations which such objects naturally excite? To the reflecting mind one or both of these must present themselves : either that the proprietor has been ruined by his improvements, or is possessed of so much blindness, as neither to feel for himself or others. When poverty, misery, and distress approximate too near the fencing which surrounds the villa, the castle, or stately mansion, these are the natural and almost unavoidable conjectures. Yet the traveller is frequently informed, that this originates in a cause widely different, and that these apparent circumstances are intended to act as mere foils, that the spectator may believe and admire with surprise, that barrenness and fertility can be so nearly allied. The contrast in many instances is very striking, and cannot fail to produce the desired effect; but, with great deference to these opinions on picturesque scenery, we beg leave to differ, conceiving that the country mansion never appears so appropriately adorned, as when surrounded by well-conditioned peasantry, and farms in the highest state of cultivation : and wherever this is the case, it is manifest that the proprietor has wisely considered, that to secure his happiness, it is essential, nay absolutely necessary, to consult the welfare and comfort of those in the

D

vicinity where he resides, and particularly that class of the community from which the very nutrition of his existence is to be derived.

For the tranquillity and future welfare of the people of these countries, it is much to be lamented that the legislature has not hitherto paid more attention to the subject of tithes, the collection of which creates so much dissatisfaction in all parts of the empire, but more particularly where the majority of the people dissent from the established church. It is said, that the late Mr. Pitt, for whose sound system of politics we are so much indebted, once had it in contemplation to lay down a plan for the commutation of them; and that the administration which succeeded him had the same object in view, to relieve our neighbours in the sister country; and it has also been insinuated, that the same subject has been thought of by those at present in power. Much would it be to their honor, and fortunate would it be for these countries, if the measure could be accomplished. Considerable pains have been taken to ascertain the state of the Protestant clergy in both islands, and it must be the sincere wish of every friend to his country, that some plan should be adopted to make a better provision for them, and to remove what is found so vexatious a grievance. There is not any doubt but the plan would be highly acceptable to the clergy, who, with few exceptions, are disposed to be satisfied. Their incomes are not always adequate to their rank and condition in life; and this is particularly remarkable in most parts of Wales, and in many parts of England, but in the sister country their revenues are in general very considerable, and where they have not so many duties to perform, in consequence of the largest proportion of the people being of a different persuasion. The tithes in that country are therefore seriously complained of, and it is the opinion of many well-informed men, that the complaints of the greatest portion of the people are not ill founded; for, independent of their own clergy, they are compelled by the ecclesiastical law to contribute their full share to the support of another establishment. It is true, that dissenters of every description are obliged to comply in like manner; but, as the people in that country are chiefly of one way of thinking upon religion, the tithe laws are more keenly felt, and therefore the people more loudly call for redress; and until some generally approved measures are adopted to alleviate their complaints upon the subject in question, it will we fear be in vain to calculate upon the time when we may hope to see the well-intentioned people in that part of the united kingdom in a state of perfect tranquillity. It is, however, absolutely necessary for the interests of the established church, that our venerable prelates and respected clergy should everywhere be maintained; yet, it is to be regretted that no mode has hitherto been discovered to bring this desirable plan to a crisis, so as to be more congenial with the feelings of those who have to pay, and at the same time less prejudicial to the interests of the people, who are without doubt materially interested in deriving as much benefit from the earth as possible; but where-tithes are taken in kind, it must prove injurious to agriculture, for although the law only allows a tenth of the produce, it is said to be one-fifth of the manure, inasmuch as it requires about two acres of straw to yield manure for the cropping of one. This may not be exactly the case in all parts of these countries, because the same mode of manuring the earth is not alike in all places, but on a general computation it is presumed to be correct. The tithe-laws, therefore, being calculated to lessen the industry of the agriculturist, must also in a certain degree impoverish the interest of the poor and industrious peasant, whose condition in society it is the interest of the nation to improve.

The peaceful and humble demeanor of the peasantry in North Britain, and their exemplary conduct in society, at once prove that no ordinary pains have been taken to cultivate their minds. They are in general well educated, sober, and industrious; and, in cases of emigration, they seldom fail by their propriety and integrity of conduct, to attract that notice which clears the way for their future promotion in life. Their habitations are much inferior to those of the peasantry of England; but, under the fostering protection of the nobility, they are verging towards improvement.

Nor can the inoffensive and hospitable manners of the Welch peasantry escape the notice of the observing and considerate traveller. Their general comforts are not much superior to those of the sister country, but their habitations are many degrees better. This however does not prove that their situation is enviable; but from the spirit for improvement which prevails, the most favorable expectations may be entertained.

By travelling through England it is impossible to help becoming tolerably well acquainted with the general condition of the peasantry, and in a partial degree, with the cause of their distress in certain districts. We shall therefore make a few cursory observations concerning them, in order to elucidate their relative situation in society, compared with the peasantry in the parts we have before mentioned, and at the same time recommend the expediency of a suitable attention being paid to the improvement of their habitations, as well as their general condition in life. In the most distressing times and under the worst of circumstances, we are convinced that ample provision is yearly made for their protection; and that distressed families may at all times be relieved by making proper application to the guardians of the poor in the different parishes where they reside. But to strangers who are not altogether unacquainted with the humanity of our laws, it appears extraordinary that so many idle persons should be seen wandering through the country in the character of regular and established mendicants. In those countries where the poor laws are not in force, it is natural to expect them in great abundance, but in a country like England, the practice cannot admit of any defence.

The subject has lately occupied the attention of our senate, and we may speedily hope to see that some wise and salutary measures will be taken to put an end to the impositions which are daily practised on the credulous philanthropist. The enormous sums which are annually collected throughout the country for the maintenance and protection of the poor, and the comfortable, and in many instances splendid establishments which are built for their reception, at once prove that the people of England are the most considerate, and perhaps the most hospitable of all the nations in the world. True hospitality consists in taking care of the poor, in protecting the aged and infirm, and in educating the offspring of the indigent, in order that they may become useful members of society. Contrast this country with any other, and where can we find, among all the nations of the earth, its equal for charitable institutions, or for its genuine hospitality? It is not only the emporium of riches and commerce, but the asylum for the distressed of all nations. Under these circumstances, therefore, it is with a pang of regret that we are compelled to observe, that the peasantry, which are the pride and boast of our country, should in any part of it be neglected. When they once become dependent on their parishes for relief, they cease to feel that honest pride which is the best incentive to industry.

Now, as the grandeur of a nation depends upon its population, it is certainly a subject worthy of consideration, that the peasantry, which constitute so considerable a portion of the empire, should be everywhere suitably lodged and provided for; the numbers which annually fall victims to disease, arising from poverty while living under the hovels we have before described, make it absolutely necessary that the greatest pains should be taken to preserve their health by promoting comfort in their habitations.

Having now, as we conceive, sufficiently shown the necessity of improving the condition of the peasantry in the manner proposed, we shall proceed to make a few introductory observations to the following designs for peasants or farmers cottages, pointing out the cheapest, best, and most approved manner of building them, under the impression that the materials of every description will be provided by the landed proprietors.

Amongst the various writers upon cottage buildings, very few of them have condescended to enter into an investigation of the present subject, conceiving perhaps that the most ordinary mechanics are everywhere equal to such undertakings as those at present under our consideration, and which is doubtless the case; but as it seldom occurs, particularly in the remote parts of these countries, that men in those humble spheres of life have been favoured with many, if any, opportunities of improving on the primitive style of building, it cannot be expected that their works will be very

E

interesting; not indeed that it is necessary to indulge in any luxuriant fancies, capricious conceits, or excursions of refined taste in the composition of designs for their habitations; but as experience tells us, that whatever has a tendency to improve the general appearance of the country, has likewise a tendency to improve the general morals, manners, and condition of the people. It is certainly worthy of some consideration to ascertain what means should be taken to infuse into all parts of the united kingdom those improvements which are the best calculated to spread their beneficial influence among the labouring classes of society; and as neatness, cleanliness, and a love of order is particularly conducive towards improving their habits, too much pains cannot be taken to inculcate such principles, and which cannot be better effected than by improving their habitations; and this we are assured, to a certain degree, is in the power of every country gentleman, who will devote only a portion of his time in attending to his own as well as to the interests of the community where he resides. From this view of the subject it is evident, that the first step towards improving the condition of the peasantry, is to promote their personal comfort, and then we may hope to see the benevolent plans laid down for their education conducive to the general interests of mankind.

Materials in building, says an ingenious writer, are like words in our language, they may be so arranged as to excite contempt, and even ridicule; but when combined with truth and expressed with energy, they actuate the mind with unbounded sway. An able writer can move in rustic language, and in like manner may a scientific builder with the rudest materials produce not only the most pleasing but enchanting effects. The peasant's cottage, therefore, as well as the palace may at all times be rendered not only an object of interest but of admiration, particularly when surrounded with picturesque scenery; and if this can be done without creating any unnecessary expence, it is a proof of good sense and discrimination in the proprietors of large estates to adopt such plans as will not only make the peasantry pleased but happy, and content in their situations, and at the same time add lustre to the country.

In the earlier ages we are informed that men lived in woods and inhabited caves; but finding these recesses damp and unwholesome, in imitation of the birds, they built huts to shelter themselves from the intensity of the weather, which they ingeniously contrived by fixing boughs of trees in the ground in a circular form, and binding them together with oziers, and covering the outside with plaster, consisting of reeds, mud, and clay. This shape being inconvenient on account of the sloping sides, the square and oblong figures were adopted, but the flat roofs being ill contrived to throw off the wet, the pointed forms were substituted, and by these means the first sort of huts, cottages, or cabins were brought to a certain degree of perfection, and from that period mankind have been continually improving, till by degrees they have been enabled to erect the most magnificent edifices; but as the present subject relates entirely to buildings of the humblest description, and for persons in the humblest walks of life, it would be superfluous to advert to any other.

Since the origin of building, considerable pains have been taken to discover the best and cheapest methods of building cottages with bricks, stones, wood, mud, and plaster; but, among the various materials enumerated, there cannot be any doubt which has the preference. Sound bricks and good building stones well incorporated with mortar of a good and binding quality, will last for centuries, while those of wood and plaster, mud or clay, are continually out of repair, and therefore ought never to be introduced in countries where better materials can be procured.

Pisan or Italian mud walls have been strongly recommended to the attention of the rural improver, but experience has taught us that they are not calculated for these inconstant climes; many attempts have been made to introduce them in various parts of these countries, but without success. At Pisa, in Italy, from which place they derive their name, they may answer the purpose extremely well, but in these moist climates, unless prodigious pains are taken in compounding the materials, and in protecting the walls against the effects of the weather, they will soon moulder away; and, as our immortal Shakespear has somewhat similarly expressed it, that like the baseless fabric of a vision, they will fall and leave not a wreck behind.

Mud walls, however, made in the common manner, with clay well tempered and mixed with sharp grit sand, will last for many years ; but as the occupiers of these tenements are frequently their own operators, the work is too speedily performed, and the consequence is, that the fruits of their labors are in most instances but of short duration, the ruinous effects of which may be seen in the different towns, villages, hamlets, and suburbs of cities throughout the empire.

For obvious reasons it is necessary that the greatest economy should be observed in the construction of peasants cottages, and for these reasons the apartments should always be on the ground floor, which will render it unnecessary to build the walls more than six, seven, or at most eight feet high, and where mud walls are introduced, the lower they are the better, in which case they should be made to batter on the outside to resist the pressure of the roof, the covering of which should project as much as possible to throw off the wet, as well as to produce effect; but, in situations where it is necessary to build them one story above the ground floor, and where the country yields but scanty supplies of hard bricks and good building stones, the skeletons of the buildings may be framed with forest timber or loppings of trees, and their outsides plastered on laths, with mud mixed with lime and chopped straw, and when dry, if promiscuously dashed with a wash, consisting of yellow ochre, lime whiting, and sharp grit sand, they will produce very pleasing and harmonious effects, particularly when constrasted with the neutral tints of shady scenery.

Walls eighteen inches or two feet thick, carefully built with common rough stones and lined in the inside with sound well burnt bricks, headers and stretchers alternately, when finished, lime whited, and the outsides rough cast or pebble dashed, are the warmest, best, and ultimately the cheapest that can be adopted in these countries, particularly in the neighbourhood of good quarries, and where bricks, lime, and sand can be procured at a moderate expence. Walls built entirely with common rough stones, are extremely cold and uncomfortable, and when plastered, unless upon battens, studding, and laths, are constantly damp. Where the materials of every description are provided by the landed proprietors, which is generally the case in England, the expence of building cottages is but trifling; for, as the peasantry by their daily employment in making and mending ditches, building and repairing walls, and making drains, are tolerably expert in the management of the spade, the axe, and the trowel, the principal part of the work in building their dwellings is performed by themselves: the facility, therefore, of thus promoting the general comfort of the peasantry in the manner proposed, may be easily effected, and by only a little attention.

As the roofs of peasants cottages are generally covered with thatch, it is necessary in the arrangement of such plans, where picturesque buildings of this sort are required, to consider what forms are the best adapted to suit the intended coverings, at the same time bearing in mind the necessity of producing as many pleasing outlines in the groupings of the roofs as are requisite to characterize the peculiarity of cottage architecture, some parts being higher than others, every part however possessing its due and just degree of interest, that when the walls of these humble mansions are reared, and the roofs put on, their general assemblage or variety of broken parts may be balanced by opposite and distinct masses of light and shade, altogether harmoniously combining with the surrounding scenery, each view presenting from the different points of sight to the preambulating spectator the most pleasing, imposing, and picturesque effects. Nor is it less worthy the attention of the rural improver who may be anxious to acquire information on our subject, to observe, that in the construction of buildings of this description, the greatest care should be taken to give sufficient pitch or elevation to the different roofs, that where they join in the several vallies they may be connected with advantage, in order that the water during heavy rains may be conveyed as speedily as possible to the places intended, without loitering on the way, and by that means obtaining time to insinuate into the thatch, which, however thick

F

or well laid, is not proof at all times against the water, under the circumstances we have mentioned, unless the declivities forming the sloping sides of the roofs are steep enough to prevent any considerable lodgment of wet, the destructive effect of which is everywhere observable in the ruinous cottages to be seen in most parts of the united kingdom; and as thatch is the warmest, cheapest, best, and most characteristic covering for the roofs of peasants cottages, and as straw or reeds of a suitable quality can be procured in most parts of these countries, we cannot conceive what apology can be offered for the introduction of either tiles or slates of any sort, which, though excellent materials for covering habitations almost of every description, are quite out of character and perfectly inconsistent upon the peasant's humble cot, particularly red tiles of any quality, which produce nearly the same disagreeable effect, as scarlet houses or cottages built with red bricks, the obtrusive and unpleasant appearance of which never fail to destroy the harmony of the most tranquil and beautiful scenery. When cottages, therefore, are built with the materials we have just mentioned, and it is desirable that they should associate with the neutral tints of the surrounding objects, they should be coloured accordingly; but where they are built with rough building stones mingled with bricks, a strong wash of lime whiting mixed with umber and sharp grit sand indiscriminately dashed on the walls, is all that is requisite to give them a rich and mellow effect when viewed with the surrounding scenery: and as the chimney-stacks appertaining to peasants cottages may be made to form very striking and interesting features rising out of the roofs, we cannot take leave of the present subject without observing on the variety of pleasing effects they produce when built diagonally, octangularly, or in groups two, three, or four together, and crowned in the manner described in the last plate.

Having studiously considered the beauties of cottage architecture, we cannot help uniting in opinion with those who have written before us, that very few parts of the most approved cottages contribute more to their exterior beauty or interior comfort than their windows: the subject is therefore worthy of some consideration, and particularly as it regards the economy of time, and consequently in a certain degree the interest of the peasantry, whose families are generally obliged to live in their kitchens between the intervals of rest; it is therefore absolutely necessary to make those rooms as large as the nature of circumstances will permit, not only for the sake of health, but for the purposes of conducting the domestic concerns of large families : in such rooms, therefore, it is desirable to obtain as much cheerful light as possible, and to take the advantage of the most pleasing aspects, in order that the occupants may embrace every moment of their time in pursuing with pleasure and profit their useful employment of spinning, knitting, or whatever is most conducive to their interest. And these rooms also, to which we have been alluding, should not only be lit by large windows, but should likewise have roomy fire-places fitted up for the purposes of frugal cookery, consisting of small grates, ovens, and boilers, so as to unite general comfort with economy in the burning of fuel. And, as few circumstances contribute more to a poor man's comfort after the toils of the day than the presence of his wife and children round the clean hearth and cheerful fire side, the greatest care should be taken in building the chimney flues to prevent their smoking, which may be easily prevented by building double flues, and making them circular within, and conical towards the top, in the way described in the last plate. And from the manner of framing and glazing the windows in the following designs, it is presumed they will be found cheaper than casement or lattice lights glazed in broad lead and fixed in iron frames, less liable to be broken, and equally, if not more, characteristic than any other description of windows at present in use for the same purpose. The apertures are of various sizes proportioned to the magnitude of the rooms, and the wood-work wrought, framed, and rebated to receive the glass, the panes of which should lap over each other, and be closely puttied in the manner of hot-house lights ; and, to give them a certain degree of interest, they should be divided about two thirds of the way up by transoms, and the perpendicular subdivisions finished with obtusely pointed heads and labels extending along the tops of the openings to divert the water trickling down the walls from running into the apertures, the further particulars of which are also explained in the last plate; and, in order to their being opened as often as required, they should be hung upon centers, which will afford the inhabitants frequent opportunities of inhaling as much fresh air as the full sizes of the apertures will admit without much, or the usual risk of breaking the glass, which is one of the evils of casement lights fixed in iron frames; besides which, they seldom fit close, and are consequently very cold, but by the windows being hung in the way described, the apartments will not only be warm, but may be ventilated with great care, which is frequently necessary where so many persons almost constantly reside. And, to add to the further comfort of these humble mansions, they should be paved with brick on edge paving laid in sand, which is much warmer and more conducive to health than any sort of rough flagging, plaster, or mud floors; the latter of which, though much cheaper, can never be made to look clean; and with respect to rough flags, though more durable, they are not so pleasant to the occupants as brick floors, which, when kept clean, make the apartments very desirable. Boarded floors for the bed rooms would be more comfortable, but in peasants cottages we forbear to recommend them, on account of the expence.

The annexed **Plate I.** represents the perspective view of a design for a peasant's or farmer's cottage, with scenery adapted to give effect to the building; the plan, elevation, and two smaller views of which are detailed in **Plate V.**: and this view is given upon a large scale, in order more forcibly to illustrate the subject in question than the elevation and smaller views can possibly produce, and will give the best and certainly the most pleasing idea of the design when executed. Perspective views of buildings drawn to small scales, are like miniatures of the human face, which, whether handsome or ordinary, seldom fail to please. To form an accurate idea therefore of the effect of any intended building, it is necessary first to contemplate the conveniences of the plan with the practicability of a well-arranged elevation, always keeping in view what the positive impression will be when reduced to practice: and to correct the judgment on this point, it is in all cases advisable to ascertain by one, two, three, or more perspective views, drawn to large and small scales, certain determined opinions, that by com-

London, Pub. March 1.1816 by R.Ackermann, 101 Strand.

Plate I.

parison the judgment may be assisted, and brought to a state of maturity. Drawings at best are but weak or specious representations of the originals: to give as just an idea, therefore, as possible of the few subjects which illustrate this work, they are drawn and redrawn to large and small scales, in order more fully to exemplify what it is conceived should characterize the contour or general appearance of these humble dwellings. A cottage too large, or a castle too small, are equally inconsistent; every building should convey to the idea of the spectator the use for which it is intended; and as we understand by the word PEASANT an humble individual, the character of his habitation should mingle with such an association of ideas as are most likely to approximate with the occupier's humble station. The lower these buildings are therefore kept the better, not only for the sake of characteristic effect and economy, but for the comfort of the occupants, whose habitations being low, they are less liable to be injured by stormy weather, which at particular seasons of the year prevail in most parts of these countries. In situations, therefore, where the ground is dry, it is sometimes advisable to descend into the apartments by five or six steps, making the window sills even with the surface of the ground. In elevated situations, and where the surrounding circumstances are favourable for diverting the water, this mode of building peasants cottages is found to answer extremely well, by which means they assume no more than their proper features in the country, and if arranged with judgment, they never cease to produce the most pleasing effects, particularly when studded among plantations of underwood or coppice scenery. Villages, hamlets, or groups of cottages built in situations of of this description on the banks of the murmuring river, or within view of the rippling stream, are the most pleasing and agreeable objects which can adorn the extended domain in the vicinity of the country mansion: and with the intention of promoting the adoption of such plans the present work has been undertaken, in the sincere hope it may at the same time produce the desired effect of improving our numerous and interesting peasantry in every part of the united kingdom.

The annexed Plate II. represents also another view of a design for a

G

peasant's or farmer's cottage, with appropriate scenery; the plan, elevation, and two smaller views of which are given on Plate VI. and this view has likewise been introduced with the same intentions as are explained in the preceding description. It will perhaps occur to those who may seriously consider the nature of our work, that the following designs have been studied chiefly to produce picturesque effects; and that the fore and back grounds, consisting of trees, &c. are introduced with the sole object of arresting the attention of persons who may not be the best or the most competent judges of building. We anticipate such observations from having been accustomed to hear them, and therefore are prepared to give our reasons for adopting this mode of giving the most pleasing effects to the designs in question. We all know by experience that drawings are more or less seductive, in proportion to their being well executed and artfully coloured; and from hence it may be justly inferred, that engravings in imitation of them will produce nearly the same effects; and for these reasons representations of the present description, it may be said, are likely to lead the mind astray; and it may also be fairly stated upon these principles of reasoning, that the views of such buildings as form a component part of this work, do not require to be treated in the manner they are, it being manifest that plantations about them are not requisite, and that therefore the perspective views and landscapes are particularly calculated to mislead; and to all these ideal objections we are in a certain degree inclined to subscribe, as far as the justice of such observations can be maintained, but, upon mature reflection, it is presumed they will be found to have little or no weight. To those who have been accustomed to travel, and have carefully watched the playful effects of nature and her fascinating powers, we think they will concur with us, that rural buildings owe many, nay, indeed most of their charms to the scenery; and that without the aid of trees, broken fore-grounds, herbage, and the surrounding circumstances, the peasant's cottage, as well as the villa, may be justly compared to a fellow-creature cast on the desert island. Trees, and the whole vegetable creation, are man's best and most innocent companions. Rural buildings, therefore, however well contrived or handsome, unless combined with their natural appendages,

London, Pub. March 1.1816 by R.Ackermann, 101 Strand.

Plate II

will neither yield pleasure or delight, and the same principle of reasoning may be applied to works of the greatest magnitude. St. Paul's Cathedral, which is so much and so justly admired for its beautiful and sublime effect, owes much of its importance and exterior grandeur to the houses which surround it ; but if this magnificent structure stood in the middle of Salisbury Plain, without any objects near it by which its magnitude and beauties could be appreciated, it would appear as uninteresting as a distant view of the pyramids of Giza on the plains of Egypt, and as forlorn as the peasant's cottage on the desert bogs of Allen. Buildings therefore of every description, whether in great cities, towns, villages, or detached from those busy scenes, should be considered accordingly, so that all the most favorable circumstances being combined, they may add to the general effect ; and the architect who does not take into his serious consideration what we have only cursorily touched upon, will labor in vain to make his designs, when carried into execution, interesting or correctly imposing. The student in architecture, therefore, who is anxious to acquire information after having studied the dry rules of his profession, should apply himself to the general study of scenery, in the pursuit of which he will discover many of the beauties of a science, the hidden mysteries of which are frequently developed by minutely reflecting upon the subjects in question. We do not mean, however, the mere copying of drawings, or the perusal of prints, but a general, close, and studious application to the works of nature, as well as the best specimens of art, which in all ages have been universally esteemed.

On the annexed Plate III. is also represented a specimen of a peasant's or farmer's cottage, with appropriate scenery, the plan, elevation, and two smaller views of which are given on Plate VII. In this, as well as the remainder of the few designs which illustrate this work, the plans are without exception irregular. Upon the principles and beauties of irregularity so much has been written by intelligent authors, that it would be a difficult undertaking to urge any thing new or interesting. Yet, as the subject is in a measure connected with what we have before written, we shall take a view of some of those buildings in which we think the architect may with great propriety deviate from the strict rules of his art, regularity in the higher orders of architecture is indispensable; but such is the prevailing taste for irregularity in modern improvements, that it is almost dangerous to propound any thing new in architecture which does not relate to irregular structures or to the picturesque in building, the ideas for which are every day creeping into our public streets, and in many parts of the metropolis, it must be confessed they have been carried into effect with no small share of success. But, indeed, to such an extravagant pitch is this desire for variety carried, that the pure principles of Grecian and Roman architecture are laid aside, and are only partially taken into consideration as mere appendages to massy buildings, but which, in many instances, are very judiciously contrived to produce the most beautiful, contrasted, and even striking effects. Designs of this description are certainly not without considerable merit; yet, not unfrequently, in proportion as they surprise they cease to please, and this takes place as the mind begins to repose, and to reflect upon the sudden causes and effects of such transitions; and this, we conceive, is a sure proof why the present taste, or rather predilection for the picturesque, should not be indulged on every occasion and in every situation, to the prejudice of the pure and genuine principles of architecture. The most correct forms and beautiful proportions are only to be found in works which unite simplicity with regularity. Buildings, therefore, which are regular in all their parts, but irregularly disposed, whether in streets, squares, or elsewhere, may create for a few seconds new and extraordinary effects, combined with the surrounding circumstances; but where designs are carried into effect, which are manifestly calculated to destroy the beautiful symetry of our best and most regular streets, we cannot help thinking that the genius of architecture has taken an excursion into the regions of fancy, intoxicated with the charms of variety. In country mansions of a certain classification, these ideas may be carried into effect with great ease, and in most instances with much propriety. Among the buildings where the principles of irregularity may be entertained, we shall notice such as are every where sanctioned by men of reputed taste. Castellated houses built in the baronice style of architecture, are much esteemed for their excellence,

London, Pub. March 1.1815 by R.Ackermann.101 Strand.

Plate III

and it generally occurs that the most admired of these buildings are irregular in their plans and combined assemblage of exterior parts. The square, the round, and octangular towers, rising out of their general masses at intermediate distances, which, intermixed with buttresses, battlements, chimney stacks, and groupings of irregular buildings, impose upon the mind very pleasing, singular, and sometimes extraordinary effects, which cannot consistently be produced in the Roman and Grecian styles of architecture; and for these reasons, in most instances the castellated mansions are to be preferred, and particularly in the mountainous parts of these islands; and we are much prepossessed in favor of this style of building in such situations, and for the best of reasons, that the bold appearances of the country in many parts of these islands, seem to favor its adoption; and without doubt it is the best calculated to harmonize with the general effects of the kind of scenery alluded to; and as stone, as well as other materials of a suitable description, can be easily procured in most parts of such countries, it will, we are of opinion, be found ultimately the cheapest, not only on account of the easy access to such materials, but as country masons are better acquainted with building stone walls than the superior sort of workmen sent from great towns, the expence of building will be much more reasonable; and where there is not any serious objection to this style of building, it ought in most cases to be preferred, as well for its grandeur as for its being the most characteristic style of residence for our ancient nobility. Gothic buildings of every description may likewise be treated in the same manner as those just adverted to: irregularity in structures of this sort, if not carried to excess, in general please. And with regard to the rustic cottage, supposed to be contrived by the uneducated peasant, nothing can be more characteristic or consistent than its irregularity, it being presumed that the occupier, who is generally the builder, is unacquainted with any but the rude principles of building, and therefore his humble mansion never appears so interesting, as when it has the appearance of being reared in the most artless manner. Chance is often very superior to design; in the consideration therefore of plans of this description, the rural architect should bear in mind the most pleasing outlines of similar buildings which have been

H

erected by the most ordinary builders, who have made convenience and necessity the first object of their thoughts : we do not mean, however, that he should copy their imperfections, but merely the characteristic simplicity of their original ideas, which, if improved upon, may frequently be made extremely interesting, and when carried into effect, add very much to the picturesque appearance of the country, and at the same time inculcate a spirit for improvement; but we have seen nothing in the various publications since our last, to induce us to give up any of our present or former ideas of the regular principles necessary to be observed in the construction of certain buildings of a superior description, intended for persons in the higher orders of life, or for public buildings. We admire, with the zeal of the painter, the leading features of the picturesque, and are fully convinced of the many truths contained in the arguments which have been very ably supported by ingenious writers upon the subject; but, whenever the ancient and approved principles of architecture are in danger of being injured by capricious ideas founded upon imaginary beauties, it is the duty of professional men to inquire into the opinions of such theorists, and to protect the dignity of a noble and most interesting science, and in the performance of which, we are induced to believe that we have done no more than our duty.

And on the annexed **Plate IV.** is likewise represented another example of a peasant's or farmer's cottage, with scenery; the plan, elevation, and two smaller views of which are explained in **Plate VIII.** In the title page of this work the reader is informed, that the following designs " are adapted for the use and convenience of the peasant and small farmer, as well as occasional retreats for persons of moderate income." It occurred to us while making the few sketches which form a part of this work, that if the plans could be contrived to answer the latter purpose, the work might prove interesting to persons who sometimes, in the neighbourhood of great towns or cities, are in want of rural retreats during a few months in the summer season; and, in order to give these designs a certain degree of interest somewhat above the habitations of the ordinary peasants, or common sort of farmers, the windows are in a slight degree ornamented, and the scenery

London, Pub.March.1.1816 by R.Ackermann, 101 Strand.

Plate IV

rather more embellished than perhaps is requisite; and this has been done that their general effects might prove in some measure equal to the expectations of persons of moderate income, who, in point of comfort, would be satisfied with one large comfortable room, and three or four bedchambers, pantry, &c. Now, as it frequently occurs that people in trade with young families residing in great cities, towns, and other places, are anxious for such retreats, it is presumed, that by fitting up the apartments in a suitable manner, that any of the following designs, with a few additions and alterations, may be made to answer as occasional retreats for small families of the description we have mentioned; and as the expence of erecting any of these buildings will be very trifling compared with the expence of such habitations as are usually erected for that purpose, we are induced to hope they will answer the intention, and be more characteristic and rural than the generality of such buildings as are termed cottages, which, independent of their being very expensive, have not the slightest pretension to that name. It may however be very justly stated, that if they are comfortable, what more can be required? It is true that, where man is content and happy, it is a matter of no consequence to him what style of building he resides in : " true happiness is of a retired nature, she haunts groves and valleys;" in which situation nothing can be more appropriate than the thatched cottage; and the citizen who seeks to enjoy peace and tranquillity from the busy scenes of life, unless his rural mansion is appropriate to the chosen situation, and to his circumstances, he will be foiled in the accomplishment of his wishes to acquire happiness in retirement. The modest trader, who retires to his humble cottage, provided the expence of such an establishment is not too great, will find as much pleasure in it as the Grecian villa or chateau of large dimensions. The truth is, that country houses are very expensive; yet it is absolutely necessary for the health of people closely confined to business, to have occasional retreats for themselves, their wives, and children, and we are of opinion that buildings of this description will answer the purpose of persons in the rank of life we have mentioned, whose plans are those of rigid economy; and cottages of the present description, with a garden and a small quantity of land to each for a cow and a horse, it is presumed will be quite sufficient. And any of the following designs, when built in a suitable manner, will not cost more than perhaps two hundred pounds, including the materials, which, if sold when complete, with the improvements of planting, will always ensure to the owner nearly the original cost. But it is necessary to observe, that the greatest economy must be attended to in building them; and, in order that such objects may be accomplished, we feel it our duty to recommend a careful perusal of the foregoing and following observations on the cheapest and best manner of building them.

Upon the annexed Plate V. is exhibited the plan, elevation, and two small views of a peasant's or farmer's cottage, the view of which is given in Plate I. to a large scale, and of which we have before given a particular description, with our reasons for the designs being drawn to large and small scales. The plan consists of one large kitchen, with three bed chambers, a large and a small closet, and, where labor is reasonable, it might be built for about thirty or forty pounds. It must however be observed, that this, as well as the following estimates, include only the workmanship, it being in all cases presumed that the materials of every description will be supplied to the peasantry by the landed proprietors, FREE OF EVERY EXPENCE; and this is inferred, because it is impossible to suppose that a poor peasant with a family can have the means, or could afford if he had those means, to lay out such a sum upon the estate of his employer. Yet, in some parts of the united kingdom, landlords are unreasonable enough to expect it, and absolutely direct the timber on their estates to be cut down, and sold to the peasants for this purpose; and this, in some degree, accounts for the miserable habitations of the poor peasants in the parts we have before adverted to. It is, however, with pleasure we observe, that this practice does not universally prevail, and that by far the greater proportion of benevolent landlords not only give the necessary materials but likewise afford every possible assistance; nay, in truth, it is the business of the landed proprietors to erect these buildings for the peasantry, and if they give up their time in assisting to erect them, it is as much, and indeed more, than ought to be expected. " The constructing of cottages for the laboring classes in society,

Plate V

Plan, Elevation, and descriptive view of a design for a Peasant's or Farmer's Cottage.

London. Pub. March 1.1816 by R. Ackermann, 101 Strand.

Scale

10   20   30   40 Feet

Bed Room
10 x 8.6

Closet

Bed Room
14 x 11

Bed Room
11 x 9.6

Kitchen
17 x 16

Closet
9.6 x 5.0

Porch

and the keeping them in constant repair are objects of the first national importance, as it is from the active and laborious exertions of these industrious people that every other class of the community derive the greatest proportion of the comfort they enjoy; it is therefore absolutely necessary that every thing should be done to encourage cleanliness among them, and to add to their personal comfort and convenience, and which, if carried into effect, in due course of time, cannot fail in all parts of the united kingdom to have the most salutary effect on their general conduct and character, and tend in a very essential manner to make them infinitely more useful in their several stations of life. It is therefore of great importance to the rich and opulent that the dwellings of their dependants should be very frequently taken under consideration, and particularly as the requisite improvements might in most instances be made with very little attention and trouble, and at a trifling expence if attended to in due time. The study of cottage scenery opens a very wide field for amusement; and in constructing or repairing dilapidated cottages, the ideas of the rural improver would be much assisted by carefully observing what has been the effect of mere chance. Necessity is frequently superior to design in the production of true characteristic simplicity; the nobility, therefore, who lay out so many thousands in improving the landscape scenery about their domains, ought never, if possible, to overlook the interesting cottage, or neglect taking into consideration the neighbouring village; for by introducing improvements on these objects, they would contribute much to their own pleasure, not only by producing the most pleasing and picturesque scenery, but at the same time add considerable comfort and pleasure to their fellow-creatures."

On the annexed Plate VI. there is also represented another plan, elevation, and two small views of a peasant's or farmer's cottage, the view of which has been given to a large scale in Plate II. The plan consists of a large kitchen, three bedchambers, a closet, and entrance porch, the cost of which will be about forty pounds. In giving our opinion of the expence, it is done with some degree of caution, it being almost impossible to form a very accurate idea of the actual expence, the value of labor differing so much

I

in every province and county throughout the united kingdom. It is therefore but fair to state, that the opinions formed upon this subject are derived by a comparative view of the price of labor, and by a general reference to precedents, and which information it is presumed is the most that can be expected in a work of this description. Estimates in general, unless made upon the spot where the work is to be done, can never be relied on. It is therefore very difficult to advise those who are about to build, unless a clew is given to the price of labor, materials, land and water carriage, as well as to the usual allowances made at the place where the work is to be done, in measuring, &c.; and this is one of the causes why estimates in general are exceeded, and sometimes it arises from the parties who build not making up their minds on the plans they have it in contemplation to pursue. Those who build are often extremely wavering in their ideas, and after they have commenced change their designs from time to time, till at length their original ideas are almost entirely abandoned. Under these circumstances it is extremely difficult to ascertain the expence before-hand; it is however always more candid and generous to state these difficulties as the alterations take place, unless there is a general building contract, in which case clauses should be introduced to protect the employer as well as the employed, by stating, that whatever additions or deductions are made from the plans agreed upon, that such allowances shall be mutually accounted for to each of the contracting parties at the conclusion of the work; and, furthermore, that no alteration or addition shall in anywise vitiate the contract; in this, and in no other way, can the architect protect the employer, the builder, and himself, from the imputation of having given perhaps indiscreet advice; and for the want of this previous and candid understanding, disputes frequently arise which might be easily avoided, and at the same time strict justice done to all parties concerned. It is a work of great labor to make accurate and detailed estimates, and it very frequently occurs, that those who make the plans are not always qualified to make the estimates; and if they should, are perhaps too indolent, and therefore employ others, who not being much interested about the event, the operation is performed in such a slovenly manner, that many very material omissions are made for the want

Plan, Elevation, and descriptive views of a Design for a Peasant or Farmer's Cottage

London. Pub.March.1.1816 by R.Ackermann 101 Strand.

Scale

10

40 Feet

Pantry
7 × 5

Bed Room
9 × 7

Kitchen
19 × 14

Entrance
10 × 5.6

Bed Room
11 × 8

Bed Room
10 × 10

Plate IV

of accurate and detailed specification, which, together with the working drawings, should all be made out before any estimate can be safely commenced. Persons therefore who are about to enter upon works of great magnitude, should not begrudge the expence of having minute estimates laid before them, with the several bills specifying the exact cost of each article, which, when done, will enable the architect and parties about to build to curtail the expence according to existing circumstances.

The making of estimates is one of the most important duties of an architect, and perhaps no duty is so much neglected; and this arises in many cases from the employer being unwilling to incur the expence of obtaining this necessary document, which is ultimately, and very frequently, seriously regretted; and, notwithstanding what may be said to the contrary, accurate estimates may be made before a brick or stone is laid. An architect, like a chymist, should be able to analyze his substances, that, as those of the profession term it, he may be able to take the whole building to pieces, and ascertain the expence before a single shilling is expended. But it too frequently happens that estimates are made by the square, the length, and breadth of the intended structure being multiplied together, and a certain sum allowed for every superficial hundred feet, and to which a price is affixed in proportion to the number of stories, and to the presumed style of finishing. This may be sufficient to give a general idea of works of a similar description, built and finished in the same manner, and in the same place, but cannot generally be relied upon; and estimators of this description seldom or ever hit the mark, and are so far wide of it, as to bring reproaches on themselves, and very often the most distressing and perplexing difficulties on all concerned.

And on the annexed Plate VII. is represented another plan, elevation, and two small views of a peasant's or farmer's cottage, the perspective view of which is given on a large scale, with scenery, in Plate III. The plan will afford accommodation for a small family, and consists of a large kitchen, with three bedchambers, a dairy, and cow shed, &c. the expence of which will be about fifty pounds. " In the construction of cottages, their situations and general outlines should be particularly attended to, in order to produce picturesque effects, where the country abounds in curved or varied outlines, consisting of hills, mountains, glens, valleys, and trees, to form their back grounds, straight or square roofs cannot be objected to ; but where the roofs are opposed to the sky, the general contour or outlines of the cottages and their perspective, from the various situations where they can be viewed, should, as it is of some consequence, be well and maturely considered. The foregrounds, as they are called by painters, or the spaces immediately before the cottages, are also of much importance to the general effect of the scenery; every possible advantage therefore should be taken of rising grounds, broken ascents, rocks, or whatever circumstances will tend to produce just and correct impressions;" for, as we have before observed, the effect of these buildings materially depend upon their situations, and, as the intelligent writer we have quoted upon the subject very justly observes, " it is with the general outlines that the effect of light and shade is closely connected, and it is upon these general principles that the entire effect of the picturesque depends. The same proportion of light and shade which is requisite in an extensive building, is by no means requisite in a small one, for when the spectator approaches so very near a large building as to be able to distinguish all its parts, the eye seldom embraces at one time much more than the body of the building itself; and for these reasons it is necessary to introduce into the front of the building, or some conspicuous part of it, an effect of light and shade, to produce a picture : but in a small simple cottage, where the eye embraces all the surrounding objects at the same time, the trees in general produce this effect. In countries, however, where they are scarce, other means should be resorted to, in order to give interest; a porch judiciously contrived, or a part of the building standing forward, will in most instances produce the desired effect."

And on the annexed Plate VIII. is also represented another plan, elevation, and two small views of a peasant's or farmer's cottage, the view of which

Plate VII

Plan, Elevation, and descriptive views of a Design for a Peasant's or Farmer's Cottage

London, Pub. March, 1.1816, by R. Ackermann, 101 Strand.

Cow Shed

Passage

Bed Room
13 × 9

Bed Room
12.6 × 7.6

Kitchen
16 × 12.6.

Pantry
& Dairy
8.6 × 7.6

Bed Room
8.6 × 7.6

Scale

10   20   30   40 Feet

is exhibited on a large scale in Plate IV. It is contrived to give suitable accommodation to a small family, consisting of a large kitchen, three bed-chambers, pantry, dairy, &c. and might be built for about forty pounds. In a former part of this work, we have alluded to what are called Pisan or Italian mud walls, and have strongly urged our reasons against their adoption; but, for the information of our readers, we have subjoined the following description of building them. " The foundation must be of brick or stone, raised about eighteen inches or two feet above the surface of the ground, and upon this foundation a moveable wooden case is fastened with wedges and common earth from the fields, which does not retain much moisture, is rammed into the case till the entire is perfectly hard. The case is then moved about as may be necessary, until the building is completed; and when the walls are dry, they are covered with a thick coat of plaster, consisting of lime and sand." Of the propriety of adopting walls of this description, we shall leave our readers to exercise their own discretion. Suffice to say, we have seldom or ever known them to answer the purpose intended, and therefore feel it our duty to caution the rural improver against their adoption. " In the construction, however, of walls for peasants or other cottages to be erected with bricks, a very great saving may be made in the materials without sacrificing much in regard to strength, by leaving the walls hollow. Hollow walls nine inches thick may be built in the following manner :---the foundations being solid, the remainder of the work may be completed by building with brick on edge on either side, every alternate brick being laid across to tie the walls together, and the cavities filled in with gravel, broken flints, or lime stones, well grouted with strong mortar; the external quoins and jambs of the doors and windows being built solid, at least eighteen inches thick, this will produce a saving in the article of bricks, and the walls being tied in throughout by chains of timber at the tops and bottoms of the windows, and by the wall plates to receive the roofs, will make the walls sufficiently strong. The divisions of the apartments may also be accomplished on a similar plan of economy, by building the walls with brick on edge, which being tied together by horizontal and diagonal inter-ties of timber, will make the divisions

K

and subdivisions complete. The chimney jambs and other walls, where absolutely necessary, should be built solid. In cottages intended for persons of moderate income near great towns, they might be thus built at a very small expence; great care, however, should be taken in building walls of this description, and that the mortar used for the purpose is of the very best and most binding quality; but in country places, where stone is plentiful, and bricks can be procured, we should recommend the walls described in a former part of this work for all sorts of rural or other buildings, which are certainly more durable than any description of hollow brick walls, or solid mud, flint, or any other sort of walls. A fourteen inch wall might also be built, with the width of two bricks laid flat, each four inches and a half wide, leaving a cavity of five inches in the middle. Bricks in width might be tied in throughout at every three or four feet, as might be found most convenient for the strength of the walls: horizontal ties of timber being also run through at the heights before described, the latter description of walls will be much stronger than those before-mentioned, but certainly not so cheap, as they will consume nearly half as many more bricks. And walls constructed in this manner eighteen inches thick, will not require so many bricks as solid walls of fourteen inches thick; and where lime is cheap, and clean gravel, broken flints, or lime stones can be procured on the spot, very strong walls may be made by filling up all the cavities in the manner before described; but no more lime should be slaked than can be immediately used, because lime soon loses a great deal of its cementing quality when kept after it has been mixed with water. Brick walls of this description will be much cheaper than solid brickwork, and if properly built, will be extremely durable." It is however but fair to observe, that they are only calculated for the use we have pointed out, and to answer plans of strict economy.

And on the annexed Plate IX. is represented another plan and elevation of two small views of a peasant's or farmer's cottage, which consists of a large kitchen and only two bedchambers, with pantry and porch, the cost of which will be about forty pounds. Hollow walls of the latter description,

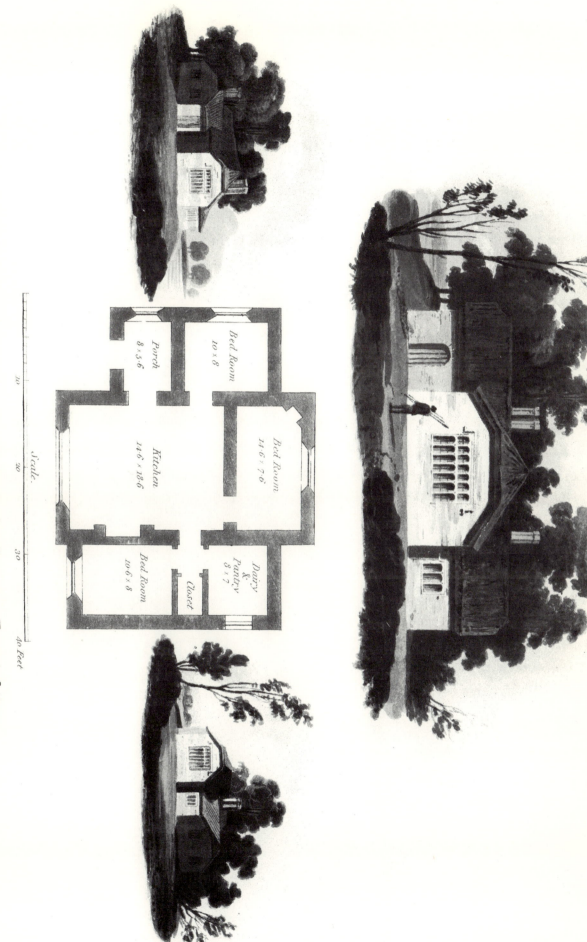

Plan, Elevation, and descriptive views of a Design for a Peasant or Farmer's Cottage.

London, Pub. March 1.1816. by R. Ackermann, 101. Strand.

Scale.

10   20   30   40 Feet

Bed Room
10 × 8

Porch
8 × 5.6

Bed Room
14.6 × 7.6

Kitchen
14.6 × 18.6

Dairy & Pantry
8 × 7

Closet

Bed Room
10.6 × 8

Plate VIII

mentioned under the head of the last plate, " being thicker than those generally built, a much better effect of light and shade may be produced in cottages, by fixing the door and window frames deeper in the walls than cottage walls will generally admit, and by these means there will be sufficient depth for inside shutters, which ought certainly to be preferred to those on the outside." We do not, however, think that folding shutters are the best adapted for the peasant's cot---flap shutters hung at the tops of the windows are no doubt more convenient, from their being more out of the way, and considerably cheaper; and we are also of opinion with the writer upon hollow walls, " that the construction of walls according to the Pisan process might be adopted, by using clean gravel flints or broken lime stones instead of common earth from the fields. Where any of these materials can be procured on the spot, and lime is cheap, it would not in our opinion be much more expensive than the simple method followed at Pisa. The gravel flints or lime stones should be composed of particles of different sizes, from the smallest-sized hazel nuts to those of walnuts of the largest size. The lime as soon as it is slaked should be mixed with water, to the consistence of thick lime wash, and then be thrown on a heap of any sort of the materials described until all the particles are wet. In this state the materials collected should be rammed into a wooden frame according to the method used in building Pisa walls, the lime being slaked and the stones mixed with it only as it is used." The hardest cements which can be found in old castle walls are composed of very sharp grit sand, and very frequently mixed with flints, small stones, and lime, only sufficient to bind the particles together. Now, if sand and gravel flints and other stones form the strongest cement, we can see no reason why the same materials will not make the strongest and most durable walls. In countries, therefore, where the materials we have mentioned are plentiful, it is worth while to try the experiment in building peasants cottages in the way last-mentioned; and as the process to be observed is simple, the workmanship might be performed by the peasants themselves. A few examples of buildings of this sort would soon spread through the country, and in a very short time in an essential degree improve their habitations. " Where flints and broken lime stones are used, care should be taken to place them as close as possible, that from their irregular shapes they may as it were dovetail or key into each other. It would," says the same writer, " be of great advantage to cottagers where fuel is dear, if the kitchens where they generally reside were to be warmed by stoves instead of open fire-places, which might be constructed of bricks, and contain a number of flues: the spaces over the fire-places being left open so as to admit small boilers, that when the boilers were not wanted, they might be covered with cast-iron plates, on which tea kettles or small pans might be boiled. Iron ovens might also be conveniently introduced, and always heated when the stoves where used. These stoves would certainly not be so cheerful as open fires, but where fuel is dear, cottagers can seldom afford to have fires to sit by." There appears a great deal of economy in this arrangement, but as a fire-side in the winter evenings creates social mirth and instructive conversation, we are of opinion that the description of fire-places explained on the last plate of this work are the best-contrived to promote comfort, and certainly better adapted to improve the condition of our peasantry, who are always more intelligent and more industrious where they enjoy the comforts of an open cheerful fire side.

And on the annexed Plate X. which is the last but one, is exhibited the plan, elevation, and two small views of a peasant's or farmer's cottage, which, with a few slight deviations, was built by Daniel Ryan, Esq. in the year 1813, in the vicinity of a mountain called the Devil's Bit, in the county of Tipperary. The plan consists of a large kitchen, with two bedchambers, pantry, and dairy, the cost of which will be about forty pounds. In describing the characteristic outlines of the roofs of peasant's cottages, we have in a former part of this work very fully given our sentiments on the inconsistency of introducing any other sort of covering than thatch, which, where straw or reeds can be procured, ought certainly to be preferred; but as it sometimes, nay indeed, frequently happens, that no other covering than tiles or slates can be procured, we shall take a cursory view of those materials which are usually adopted as substitutes, and unite our own with the opinion of other writers upon the subject. There are but two sorts of

Plate IX.

Plan, Elevation, and descriptive views of a Design for a Peasant or Farmer's Cottage

Bed Room
11 × 5

Bed Room
11 × 8

Kitchen
20 & 16

Pantry
10 × 5

Lobby

Scale

10   20   30   40 Feet

London, Pub. March 1, 1805, by R. Ackermann, 101 Strand.

tiles which are made in these countries for dwellings or other buildings. The one sort are called plain or flat tiles, and the other sort are called pan-tiles. Pantiles are the cheapest, but in consequence of the strong lines of light and shade produced by their twisted forms, the roofs covered with them attract too much attention; the neat, snug, and compact style of plain tiling upon a cottage roof has a much better effect. The objection, however, to tiles of either of the descriptions mentioned upon cottages is their colour; these tiles however are sometimes coloured with quick-lime, sharp sand, and soot mixed together with water. This composition produces a grey colour not unpleasant to the eye; but for picturesque cottages intended to harmonize with rural scenery, we should prefer something in imitation of brown thatch a few years old. In some parts of the kingdom, particularly in the north riding of Yorkshire, the tiles are glazed of a dark lead colour, but the effect they produce is not equal to our wishes. Grey slates of a moderate size have rather a handsome appearance on cottages, and in some places may be procured much cheaper than any other sort of covering, and this is particularly the case in most parts of North and South Wales, and in some parts of the sister country. Blue slates may likewise be procured in many other parts of these islands, " but we have seldom or ever seen them introduced to advantage on cottages; their cold plain colour is not calculated to harmonize with picturesque scenery, except when inclined a little either to a rich brown or to a greenish colour somewhat resembling our Westmoreland slates. Red tiles, therefore, in most cases are to be preferred to blue slates, as the tiles, from the roughness of their surface, may be coloured to stand a considerable time, and in the vicinity of trees they will soon acquire moss and weather stains, which will make them blend with the harmonizing tints of rural scenery. There are various methods of colouring tiles as well as walls, but the durability of the colour depends in a considerable degree on the materials being made rough to retain it---coarse bricks answer this purpose extremely well." For colour-ing red or any other sort of bricks, we have before given some general hints; but as we are anxious to give our readers as much information upon the subject as possible, we have subjoined the following opinion of an intelligent writer on the subject, who says, " For colouring coarse or rough bricks, we should

L

recommend the best stone lime immediately after it has been slaked and sharp grit sand mixed with water, and coloured by means of lamp or ivory black and yellow ochre ; what is called blue black, and prepared from charcoal, ought perhaps to be preferred ; where good quick lime cannot be procured, lime or whiting, and the same colour may be mixed with the liquor of boiled linseed. This colour will last for a long time upon bricks or tiles." Any colour, however, is better than red bricks, tiles, or walls approximating to whiteness : in rural scenery they have just the same disagreeable effect as they have in pictures, in the composition of which landscape painters carefully avoid the glaring effects of either. The common sort of stucco is also very frequently applied to brick cottages, and if well and carefully executed, is almost as durable as some kinds of free stone. The lime should be of the best quality, and be used immediately after it is slaked, and the sand ought to be as clean as possible, and the particles of the largest size. The proportion of lime to the sand will depend on the quality : in general, two portions of sand to one of lime is deemed requisite. In some parts, however, where the lime is of a superior quality, three portions of sand to one of lime is introduced, and this is the case in most parts of the sister country, where the lime as well as the land in general is much superior to the generality of our English soil. " For cottages, a single coat of this stucco laid on with an uneven surface, to give it the appearance of undressed stone, will produce the desired effect, and look much better than colouring or the common sort of rough-cast, or what in some parts of the kingdom is called pebble-dashing. In many parts of the country the walls of cottages are first plastered, and then stuck with irregular stones about the size of small nuts. This is what the Italians call PARRETTA work, and we believe it is known by that name in most parts of these countries. It has a very pleasing appearance, and not only adds very much to the durability of the walls, but to the comfort of the inhabitants, as by this means the walls are kept constantly dry, and of course the apartments are much warmer."

And the annexed Plate XI. which is the last, exhibits the detail of one of the cottage windows in the foregoing designs, on a large scale, so as to pro-

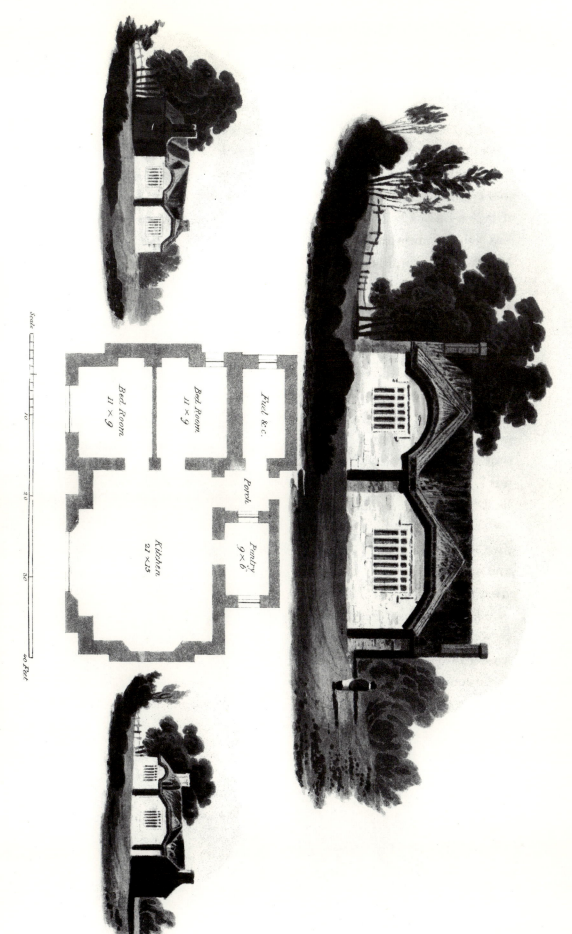

Plan, Elevation, and descriptive view of a design for a Peasant's or Farmer's Cottage.

London, Pub. March 1 1816 by R. Ackermann, 101 Strand.

Plate X

Scale

10
20
30
40 Feet

Bed Room
11 × 9

Bed Room
11 × 9

Fuel &c.

Porch

Kitchen
21 × 15

Pantry
9 × 6

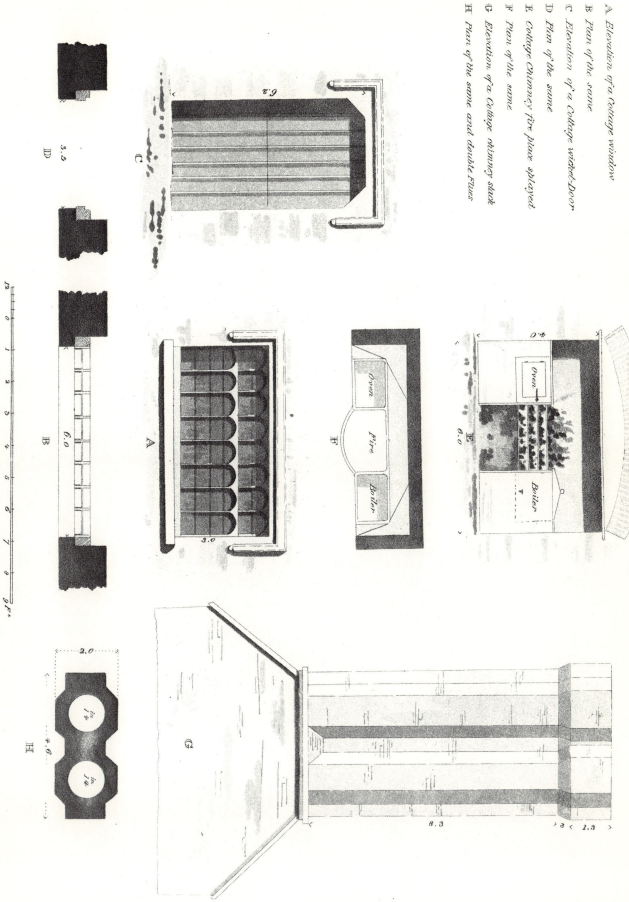

Reference

A. Elevation of a Cottage window
B. Plan of the same
C. Elevation of a Cottage wicket-Door
D. Plan of the same
E. Cottage Chimney fire place splayed
F. Plan of the same
G. Elevation of a Cottage chimney stack
H. Plan of the same and double Flues

Plate XI

London, Pub. March 1.1815 by R.Ackermann, 101 Strand.

duce the general effects represented in the elevations and views, without incurring the expence of iron frames, with lead lights ; the particular manner of finishing which we have before described. This plate also illustrates the most characteristic manner of finishing the stacks of cottage chimnies, with the most approved and economical manner of building and fitting up the kitchen fire-places, so as to unite general comfort with economy in burning of fuel, and likewise the most approved and characteristic style of finishing external cottage doors. Having now given, it is presumed, sufficient information on our subject, we shall conclude the foregoing hints by observing, that wherever the peasants cottages are in a state of ruin, surrounded by filth, pigsties, and other buildings equally prejudicial to health, that they never fail to inspire misery; and that where this is the case, it is the surest proof that the morals, manners, and habits of the occupiers correspond with the surrounding circumstances. Yet it is singular that in many parts of the united kingdom their local aversion to decency is so great, and this arises for the want of due care and attention being paid to their condition, that a poor cottager would be ridiculed by his village friends for being more decent and cleanly in his general habits than his neighbours.

The improvement of the peasantry opens such a boundless space for the researches of the human mind, that it would be extremely difficult to prescribe to it any limits. To accomplish so desirable an undertaking upon a grand scale, it would be necessary to enter into a minute investigation of the local interests of the people throughout every province and county in the united kingdom; but as such views cannot be comprised in a small work of this description, we must content ourselves with having pointed out the necessity of improving their condition, as far as relates to their habitations, trusting that the ulterior advantages to be derived by taking into consideration their personal comfort, may at no distant period be productive of general good to the empire at large.

FINIS.

PRINTED BY FRANCIS MARSHALL,
31, Kenton Street, Brunswick Square.

ERRATA.

Page 1,—*for* " considerate interest," *read* " considerable interest."

20,—*for* " great care," *read* " great ease."

24,—*for* " symetry," *read* " symmetry."

—,—*for* " baronice," *read* " baronial."

31,—*for* " should not begrudge," *read* " ought not to think much of the expence."

DIRECTIONS TO THE BINDER.